GETTING TOGETHER
OR BREAKING UP

Getting Together or Breaking Up

The Dating Man's Guide to Understanding More About Women (or Almost Doing So)

Jeff Redmond

Writers Club Press

San Jose New York Lincoln Shanghai

Getting Together Or Breaking Up
The Dating Man's Guide to Understanding More About Wormen,
or Almost Doing So

Writers Club Press
an imprint of iUniverse.com, Inc.

For information address:
iUniverse.com, Inc.
620 North 48th Street, Suite 201
Lincoln, NE 68504-3467
www.iuniverse.com

ISBN: 0-595-12662-6

Printed in the United States of America

List of Contributors

The author would like to thank the following for their helpful assistance with this book: Judy K. for her patience, Lori M for her info about iUniverse, Bonnie K. for being such a good role model, Madelyn G. for her photographic skills, Andrea W. for her alternatives, Becky A. for her literary persistence, Heidi L. for ideas, Mai T. for her knowledge of other cultures, Debbie M. for her videos, Mira L. for her lunches, Cathy R. for her editorial power, Kelley R. for her comments and criticisms, Amy S. for her artistry, Jodi W. for her wisdom, Charlotte W. for her networking, Beth B. for her theatrics, Jeanne R. for her capabilities, Mary P. for her sincerity, Sue B. for her experiences, Patty D. for her initial interactions, Jenna M. for her information, Chris G. for her camera work, Connie M. for her club membership, Cindy H. for her time, Carol C. for her introductions, Susan P. for her invitations, Celeste S. for her dinners, Mary Jane K. for her spontaneity, Joan D.P. for her trips to the beach, and the many other women I have learned so much from.

Contents

Introduction

In my many years of dating experiences, what has fascinated me most is the way things can turn out. I have had to learn about all the sub-conscious psychologies, hidden agendas, and secret desires of people dating. Being male I was, of course, strongly motivated by sexual attraction. But it was way more than that. A lot more! And it was too terribly confusing for me to allow to go uninvestigated. My sex life was 90% fantasy and only 10% reality (if that). I decided to do something about my personal hetero-sexual male ignorance.

I have spent long hours reading, researching, and studying up on the problem. After two decades of being 15 to 35 years of age, interacting with females from fourteen to forty, and succeeding or failing for all sorts of reasons, here are many of my findings. You too can begin to get good at almost understanding women.

Beginning definition: MULIEBRITY (the state of being a woman)

I

Confusions

I'm a basic guy just like you. There's nothing at all spectacular about me. I'm not a millionaire, never been a sports hero, nor a famous rock or movie star. I dated and failed with more girls than I can remember, and all because I didn't really understand them. Looking back on my past years, I've finally decided to collect together all the things about women I've been able to learn. And especially the lessons from all the dates that didn't work out the way I intended them to. I'll never forget the words of the one blond haired and blue eyed Swedish girl. She was Suzanna-Birgitta, the one I took out enough times, but who didn't let me have sex with her.

She told me, "If you'd been more insistent I would have let you."

Another time I had an attractive and educated American lady over for a rather romantic dinner. I waited on her, filled her with wine and gourmet food, and kept myself patient and attentive with her. Then she surprised me by politely thanking me for the meal, getting up, and putting on her coat.

She told me, "I'd spend the night with you, but you're too nice."

And she left.

In the modern dating scene expectations often go unrealized. Both boys and girls are disappointed with the way their social life is going. This may be because of the failure to communicate. In interviews with numerous socials we asked young males and females in their late teens and twenties what the date rate is currently at.

Jocelyn, 24, is a brunette substitute teacher, single, with no steady boyfriend, and has not gone out with in quite a while.

"I've been celibate for over two years now", she says.

"Do you still socialize with girlfriends?" we asked her.

"I tried licking lesbianism for about five minutes, but gave it up for good."

"Why do you still prefer men, then?"

"Because they have a dick!" Jocelyn says. "Although it's NOT the size but how they use it that counts."

Jodi, blond and 21, is a waitress, single, and also in no steady relationship.

"All the guys I know are so immature!" she complains. "They ask me out but don't even try to get me in bed. One of them didn't even want me to go down on him!"

Cyndi, 19, an attractive green eyed art student, agrees with her.

"I go out with a really hunky dude and really get turned on by him. I think he's a real studmuffin and get moist, and suggest we go to my place, but they just clam up and get all crapped out cold and distant on me. So he ends up being a real asshole!", she says.

The males seem to be having the same kinds of problems in unrealized expectations. Don, 20, an office worker, complains about his dates.

"I asked this one young lady to meet me for lunch, but she wanted to have a dinner instead. When I didn't suggest that we spend the night together she asked me if I was gay! Yeah I'm in shock. How else can I be?" he says.

"The girls today have lots of boyfriends, and don't want to stay with just one", says Mark, 26, a repairman. "I'd really like to get a nice girlfriend and eventually get married, but can't really connect with them."

Don, 31, asks, "How come the same woman will act so sexy and slutty all around the guys, but will always put on the sweet innocent virgin act when she's with other females?"

There are definite indications of trends away from traditional male and female interactions, and young people today often express their bewilderment and confusion about what it is exactly they should be, want, and do.

"Times have changed, and socializations have altered along with it", says Dr. John Zaugra, student counselor at Grand Valley State University.

"We find from interviews and studies that both males and females are experiencing difficulties adapting and adjusting to their new roles.

Dr. John Mailesom of the Social Work Program at Western Michigan University identifies some major reasons why.

"There are several factors at work in out modern society", he says.

"These include the Feminist Movement, more women than men in college classes and in the workplace, modern birth control, the breakup of families, decreasing parental and religious organizational controls, and increased mobility for women to travel and seek their own independence and careers."

Barbara Clayton, a psychotherapist at Price Family Counseling in Grand Rapids, identifies other factors as well.

"Young women come to me all the time complaining about how seemingly uncaring and unromantic the young men are. I try to help them identify their own personal attitudes and behaviors which cause others to react to them in these ways."

"The so called Womens' Liberation has not always been the best as hoped for women in our society", says Randy Flood, a counselor at the Psychological Consultation Center of Pine Rest Mental Health Services. "It has virtually ended our traditional values of romance, and also lowered females somewhat down to the worst of the behaviors of males. This is why so many girls today are acting and expressing themselves in what was once considered such crude and vulgar ways. They think that they have to behave just like men supposedly are, and all because of peer pressures and expectations for sexual equality with men."

Michelle, 19, a red headed actress and model, also expresses herself in a similar way: "The chicks I know don't have the right equipment to screw me, and the gay guys I know don't want to. So that leaves the straight guys, but they don't even try. Maybe I'm too aggressive and intimidate them. But they're such wimps! I get so horny, but they don't even try to seduce me!"

Males are also experiencing unprecedented role reversals, as social attitudes and behaviors rapidly change.

"There is a new awareness in younger males to be more sensitive to a female's opinions and needs", says Charlene Wickering, a social worker at Holistic Counseling. "But the men in my classes tell me that they're often having difficulties finding any kind of traditional mating material to bond and settle down with. Marriages are down and divorces are up in statistical trends. Dating and courtship obviously isn't what it used to be."

"I'm scared to flirt with or ask any girl out at work", says Ethan, 17, a part time clerk and stock boy. "If you say or do one little thing wrong they try to get you for sexual harassment. I mean, I like them, but sometimes I'm afraid of them!"

"The girls at school just don't make any sense", says Nate, 18, a highschool senior. "If you act too cool and treat them badly they love it, but if you act polite and friendly to them they just aren't interested at all. If I don't have a girlfriend I can't get any, but if I do suddenly get one then there's all these other ones coming on to me. It's like feast or famine or something."

There seems to still be genuine needs to interact with members of the opposite gender, especially in ways over which we can express and fulfill our innermost desires.

"Sales of Romance fictional novels has skyrocketed in the past years", says Paul B., 26, a manager of a Bargain Books store. "And these are exclusively to younger and middle aged ladies. We had dozens of sad and lonely single gals in here last Valentine's Day, and almost all of them bought two or three Romance paperbacks each. And now we even get guys coming in here to buy some."

Such books and stories are certainly filled with an abundance of heaving bosom heroines and bodice ripping male characters. Many are just non-stop crude and foul page after page of blatant sex. But some also deal with real life problems and situations women face, and these especially include isolation and loneliness from adequate connection and communication with a suitable man. Males often suffer from the same problems, but turn to more visual outlets for their limitations and frustrations.

"We get a lot of older married guys in here, but a lot of younger single guys too", says Lyle K., a manager of a Starz Unlimited Adult Video store. "They want to spend time with an attractive fantasy girl who will make up for all the lack of one they have in real life. And lately we've been getting more and more women in here to check out our X-rated videos for themselves, too."

Sales and rentals of adult videos has tripled in the past decades in the area, and show no signs of diminishing. The communication gap between males and females, or females and males, seems to not be diminishing.

So what can be done to improve social interaction and the date rate?(Click here to input your first chapter title and/or number, if any.)

II

Influences

Females get most of their education about boys, men, and dating from the womens' magazines and advice columnists. A good way to learn about what they are learning about is for you to also read these articles.

The public libraries always have such magazines in their periodical sections.

So do the waiting rooms at the doctor's or dentist's offices. And so do the supermarkets. I always get in the longest checkout line and grab a magazine or two to brush up on the latest in "feminine self-help" information. More than a few smart women, especially in publication and advertising, make money off of their fellow females' insecurities. They market to convince girls that their young lives will be so much better if they spend their earnings on the products advertised in the media.

These always have ads for hair care, makeup, clothes, jewelry, weight loss and any other kind of thing helping to improve their appearances.

There's also all kinds of drivel about movie star and fashion model gossip, recipes, scandals, latest fads in entertainment, and the like. All this makes up about 90% of each publication, so narrowing your field of focus to the remaining 10% of actual articles makes it much faster and easier. These almost always deal with women trying to interact with men, and are mostly female complaints and criticisms about why men are not perfect, etc.

But every once in awhile there's a really useful and relevant article that will pertain to your particular situation. And these are what you can learn important information from, and all with the woman's "secret" point of view. I've found the very best to be the "tips" on how to handle men.

I almost always immediately pick up on what a woman is actually trying to say to me, just from her word usage and meanings, which is easy to tell if it comes directly from her reading these advice features.

There's an old saying that men run the world, and women run the men who run the world. (Look at our past presidents). Females feel that they live in a male dominated system, and that they always need to manipulate the men they associate with in order to get things done "correctly" (which is always THEIR own way). They will seldom apologize or give in, unless we do so first. After hundreds of generations and thousands of years of evolutionary development, it's a game they learned from their mothers, who got it from their mothers, about handling their fathers, husbands, sons, etc. These almost always work, and so they are still used.

Girls go to schools in an American education system copied from one established in England in the 18th and 19th centuries. Back then only sons of the aristocracy went to colleges, and then only to learn how to be gentlemen. Classes included foreign languages, literature, and the history of men fighting wars. Modern additions to curriculum have included math, science, engineering, and now computers. Do women want or need to learn these kinds of things? Most do not. They often take classes in art, music, theater, poetry, nursing, and elementary school education instead.

In the modern American society teenagers are expected to remain younger than "adults" in expectations of a prolonged adolescence. They date and go to social events, but usually do not mate and marry until they are years older. American girls often prefer to be talked to as if they were a child, as this is what they are used to, especially from men. This also frees them from any of the responsibility of having to be accountable for their own actions. Many girls still prefer to be taken care of, even with all the counter influences of modern Feminism. The American culture idolizes the romantic notions of the Southern belle, in her plantation mansion, being courted by gentlemen vying to win her hand. Almost all American girls have this fantasy at one time or another.

Our modern media controlled society constantly broadcasts the epitome of the "perfect" female being a model. To many American women this is what they themselves wish they could be. They see the famous ones being admired, glorified, desired, and paid attention to by so many men. The less than "perfect" females envy and are even jealous of these model types. Another great influence on American society are our highschool systems. These are far more athletic and social than academic, and they provide such things as Homecoming and Prom dances for status seeking teenagers to attend. Just as almost every highschool boy would like to date that gorgeous cheerleader, so almost every girl longs to be the date of that football hero.

Many women who are attractive and intelligent will remain with men who use them and treat them badly. These kinds of females have low self esteem, or desperately hope that they can somehow ultimately get these badly behaving males to change for the better (even though this seldom happens).

There are also women who are attracted to men but afraid of sex. These kind hang around with gay guys and quickly become known as "fag hags."

Girls who have known each other all through elementary and junior high schools, been best friends and constant companions, will suddenly turn on each other in highschool. They will fight viciously and remain bitter enemies for the rest of their lives. Why? Usually because they both liked the same high status boy at the same time for the same reasons. Females learn at a very young age how to be attractive to males, and also how to be competitive to win against other females. They can be very, very nasty with each other. A woman needs constant reassurance of her appearance, your affection, and that there is a lack of competition from other females. And they all know how to get it. When it comes to men, most women play The Game to win!

III

Motivations

When you're out on a date with a girl and she whines, cries, pouts, teases, complains, argues, acts super sexy, gets cold, gets warm, laughs, or just about anything else, she's doing it all to control you. One of the things she wants most is to be noticed, and she will do just about anything to get and keep it. Her strength is in her ability to almost always get you to give this to her, but it is also her great weakness.

Because almost all other women want and need the same thing. And there's three females for every two "suitable" males out there. With so many guys in jail, overseas in the military, gay, on drugs, too young, too old, or too weak the numbers advantage is in the mens' favor. So when a girl suddenly starts wiggling around, playing with her hair, and acting more extroverted near to you, it's because she wants your Attention.

Women often rely on the opinions of others about themselves, and seldom have minds of their own in this regards. All women aged fifteen to thirty-five or so are always aware of their biological clocks. This means their chances of meeting and marrying the "perfect" man diminish as they get older, near menopause, and are no longer able to reproduce. And this, despite all the feminist clamor otherwise, is precisely what most women want to really concern themselves with. They see how happy new mothers are, envy their married sisters and female friends, and idolize male rock and film stars as perfect husbands and fathers of their children. Almost every woman's publication includes the all important fact about whether or not a famous man is married or single. Women thrive on attention and Relationships.

When you are out on a date with a girl, and she decides to relax and trust you enough (or just a little), she'll slowly but surely start to reveal her true self. If you are eating she'll talk all about how food is a domestic pastime. She may, if she's a traditionalist, tell you all about what a good cook she is. If she's a feminist type she may say that she can't cook since her career is "more important" etc. But she may also say this in a slightly insecure way, almost as if she wishes otherwise. She'll want to get or want to give you food, candy, or something else to eat. This is because of her needs for Domesticity.

If you go to a zoo or animal farm, or especially pet shop she'll always want you to see her hugging the soft and cuddly creatures. She'll loudly make a big and happy fuss about how much she likes kittens or puppies or hamsters. This is done deliberately to let you know how nurturing she can be with her future babies. She'll be watching you closely to see how you interact with other peoples' kids. Are you good marriage and/or father material? This is all about her needs for Maternity.

On a walk past a jewelry store or dress shop, she will almost always want to stop and admire the merchandise, with you seeing her do so. She is letting you know that her appearance is important, and the more expensive items make her look and feel the most attractive, feminine, sensual, etc.

If you spend money on her then she is important to you, and you care about her, and she can feel confident with you. The more wealth, status, fame, position, and power you have the better you can protect her, provide for her and her children, and take care of her. They crave hugs from you, and they are always perfectly contented when you cuddle up and hold them. Women usually desire men who are older, taller, and wealthier. These men can better take care of them during their pregnancies. The feminists try to deny this, but thousands of years of evolution have proven it to be true.

This deals with her needs for Security. When you are out with a girl you will notice that suddenly many other females start looking, smiling and even flirting with you. If you were out by yourself none of them would bother at all with you. Your date will get reactive and grip your arm harder, or interrupt you more frequently, or even get overly provocative with you. They always worry about and always suspect that you are interacting with other women. You can have no girlfriend at all for months, and then suddenly have two or three at once.

"Feast or Famine" certainly applies to dating, and the females all know this. One ex-girlfriend used to even call me four or five times each day, just to check up on me. This is because she's always aware that there's many other single, lonely and desperate females out there. This is because of her feelings about Competition.

A woman's ultimate game with men is their ability to reproduce or not reproduce. This is why the feminists rampage so about abortion rights, and why popes continue to refuse women the sanctions to use birth control.

A baby is what a woman (as a Man with a Womb) is ultimately all about. She will be most contented keeping up with the other rival females by getting pregnant. A husband is the highest status for her too, and this is why a female who gets engaged suddenly lords her ring and wedding plans over all the other females. This is why the still single girls at weddings get so excited about the bridal gown, and so nasty and catty in their remarks about the bride. Sex is their Power.

For a woman having a man in her life enhances her existence thoroughly.

She has a friend and companion, someone to get to do things for her, and someone to help her take care of her living expenses. Even the successful career women want men to buy them gifts and take them out to dinners. A man with a new car, a famous name, an important title, a powerful position, money, book authorship, song recording, film acting, television show appearance, or whatever is a real find for her. He is someone and something that she can brag to all her girlfriends and female co-workers about. A man is her Status.

IV

Getting Going

So what can you do to first attract a mate? I found that looking nice, acting nice, and being nice all help, but don't really do much on their own. The best way to meet women is through other people. Females, out of obvious necessity, do not trust men who approach them when they are alone.

They are vulnerable and defensive, and are afraid of all too real attack, rape, mugging, kidnaping, assault, etc. A woman really appreciates it when her female friend or colleague introduces her to some "suitable" (eligible) man. They operate through a network of human contacts and relationships.

Women will ask others who know you all about you, and they will try to find out all they can about you in advance.

You can utilize this same network, and also help increase the status of woman who "finds" you for other women to admire. They each love being Queen Bees with a hive full of male drones around them, and especially with a few extra males to pair off with the other females. This accomplishes two things at once. It both helps out her fellow females in finding mates, and cuts down on competition from them for her own man selection, at the same time. Women like, but do not completely trust each other, ever. If a girl does not get along at all with her mother, she will feel especially competitive with other females. If a girl lacks a father in her life, due to death, divorce, or whatever, she will be especially desirous of a man in her life. Often girls will marry older men to fill a Daddy role in their lives, and they will fight off other females for him tooth and nail.

How do you get a girl to go out with you? The only way is to ASK!

Every heterosexual female wants to date a male, and especially a higher status one. But almost none of them ever make the first move and ask the guy out. They may hint at things, get their girlfriends to suggest to you to do so, or even include you in an invitation to a party. But for all sorts of the reasons mentioned above, girls want you to be attracted to them, pursue them, attain and win them, and so forth. Women thrive on fantasies of being abducted and carried off by Mr. Right, or of being able to get a slightly less perfect male to alter his behavior and change just for them. Phone calls, letters, cards, gifts, flowers, candy, and any other kind of "surprises" will certainly all help. Women have needs for continuous Romance.

Once you've been dating, and going out together more than just a few times, she may start to make some suggestions as to where and what you two should go and do. She will let you make all the arrangements and ideas for the first few times. This is so she can get more ideas and information as to what you are really all about. She will be paying attention to what you say, how you say it, how you behave, and your attitudes and opinions about things of most importance to her (like HER). She may help pay for some of the date, or drop hints about what she likes and dislikes, but basically it is up to you for the first few times. You are, after all, supposed to be the MAN protecting her, respecting her, courting her, and winning her.

V

Getting In

Slowly but surely she will begin manipulating you, fine tuning you to fit in more perfectly with her needs and desires, and getting you to change just for her. This is both good and bad, as it gives you more of a comfortable and responding her to be with, but also makes you aware of all the things about you that she doesn't like. Still, in the end, women can and do make it all well worthwhile. After enough dates it will be time to decide whether or not to get completely intimate, and this means getting her into bed.

Once a relationship has reached the sexual intercourse stage, the most hidden factors come into game play. You have been attentive, respectful, and persistent long enough to get sexual release through coitus. She has been attractive, desirable, and provocative enough to get you to prove yourself to her. She is allowing you to have her in order to achieve her needs for emotional intimacy and security with a naked man on and in her.

Her "job" in bed is to please and satisfy you, while yours is to make her feel the most adored, loved, and safely secure. This is why women get so upset if after sex the man leaves, goes to sleep, watches the game on TV, or whatever. She wants and needs him to continue to hold and caress her, and even (after he's rested up a bit) go at it again. This is because of each and every woman's needs for Love.

She will "allow" and "permit" you to get her into bed, while at the same time make you think it's all your idea. She will try to be both a virgin and a whore simultaneously, while being sexy enough to get and keep you, but not overdoing it to become too much of the one maliciously gossiped about by the other females she knows. Whatever and regardless of this, she's still naked, warm, turned on, and yours exactly where you want her to be. A bubble bath and body oil massage first will really help things along, as will a candlelight dinner, soft music, and some kind of a gift. Whereas males are more Visually orientated by what they see, females are way more Auditory in what they hear, sense, and pick up on.

This is why when you are out on a dinner date you notice her legs and cleavage, as well as those of the other girls showing off at the other tables. This is also why she is noticing the soft lighting, the candles, the music, the atmosphere, and especially reacting to the tone of your voice. You might be boring her silly with your monologue about the sports game you enjoyed, but she still feels so much more happy and contented when she is out with you. One of her worst fears is being left home alone. She appreciates the chance to be out somewhere. Even better for her is when she discovers that other females she knows see her there. Best of all is if you are a high status male, and they tell everyone else all about her being with you. It made her day!

Men dress for success in more uniform ways which define their roles of occupations and positions. Police, soldiers, sailors, sports athletes, and postal workers all wear various types of uniforms. Business executives need their suits and ties to fit in with others they work with. Men have almost always had dress codes to follow. Women wear the female equivalent of these whenever they enter the work world, but no woman wants to be caught dead in the exact same dress as another one is wearing at a party. Women will notice another woman's clothes, while men will notice what's inside the clothes. Females are also told in their womens' magazines that they need to dress in certain ways for different situations. And so they do. But they also keep us guessing.

How they wear their hair, up or down, long or short, colored or natural all says a lot about what mood and situation they are in. According to surveys only 5% of blonds are naturally so, and most older women do everything they can to hide their gray hairs. The shorter the skirt the more she is advertising her legs and her potential reproductivity. If she has on a sports jacket with broad "power" shoulders she's trying to emphasize her office abilities. A woman wearing a combination of both of these (and we've all seen these types out there) is obviously sending mixed signals about themselves. They are perhaps confused about themselves and what they want, a husband or a career, a baby or a promotion, etc.

Studies done of young single women at discos correlated their dress style with their menstrual cycles. The closer to ovulation the less clothing covering their bodies. Shorter skirts, bare arms, bare backs, higher heels, more makeup, etc. The closer to menstruation the less body exposed, and long pants, long sleeved shirts, and less makeup were more common. Their cycles also strongly influence their moods, with ovulatings causing increases in estrogen and more feminine and mating ritual behavior.

PMS and menstruating times are what we'll just have to put up with and wait out, and not at all necessary to be discussed here.

VI

Controls

Whereas males in societies are kept in line more by external factors, females are more controlled by internal ones. Men have such things as police, courts, jails, laws, bouncers, coaches, drill sergeants, and other elements to make them behave. Women have their own feelings of guilt, worries about what others will say about them, and their own beliefs in proper behavior to all influence what they say and do. Males in all societies organize themselves in linear power structures, with authority figures at the top giving orders, rewards, and punishments down the chain of command. Females almost always organize themselves into groups of equally sharing and empathic interaction with one another, while coping with these male power structures at the same time.

With both such external and internal controls constantly upon the population, it's no wonder that males in general are frustrated-especially sexually. Pornography, computer sex, and masturbation are rampant in the underground of our system. Females in general are repressed-especially sexually, along with inhibitions, insecurities, and their unfulfilled needs for romance. The modern United States has a very neurotic society with many aspects, rules, and expectations left over from the Puritans and Victorian Age traditions of our culture.

Modern Feminism has sometimes tried to remedy this, but often not.

Many of the feminist leaders and writers are White, upper middle class, university educated, liberal, lesbian, and far removed from the mainstream masses of women in America today. Few women in the U.S. realize just how well off they are materially, socially, and legally compared with the vast majority of the world's population-especially female. American women, and especially White ones, do not realize how envied and even despised they are by so many others of minorities and in the Third World countries.

A White girl just out of college in the U.S. today, complaining about having to drive last year's model car, or not being able to immediately be the C.E.O. of a major corporation, is laughed at by these other ones. Girls in their later teens in Third World countries are often married, raising young children, and trying to survive wars, plagues, and famines. Girls of the same ages in the U.S. are struggling to decide about which dress to wear to a Homecoming dance, or which university daddy will pay for them to go to (if they decide to bother to do so). In America females face two diametrically opposing points of view, and they have to cope with both on a daily bases.

The first is that men want them to be attractive, desirable, sensual, sexual, and even somewhat slutty. Girls thus wear makeup, hairstyles, and provocative clothing to attract, entice, and impress males. But the second and opposite point is the influences of other females upon them. Older women dislike sexual competition for men from younger women, other girls gossip viciously about them, and mothers raise their sons to not want to really marry and reproduce with females who are not virginal. Therefore females must negotiate their way through these two extremes, and thus they often have to lie and be deceptive about what they want, need, and do.

Girls who are smart will often act as if they are dumb, and visa versa.

Ones who are virgins will often try to look and behave as if they are whores, and visa versa. Many females feel guilty and "dirty" for wanting to be sexual and actually being so. Some of them will even refuse to date a man who is "too nice" because they believe they should have sex with a fellow who is himself "not nice." Sex in American culture is something negative. Nudity, pregnancy, copulation, etc. have all been repeatedly attacked and condemned by church and "moralistic" groups. The underground sex industry certainly continues to thrive.

Women thus feel that they need to be and remain mysterious in order to survive in this kind of social system. They often blame men for maintaining a "double standard" of behavior where it's all right for males to be sex crazed barbarians, but females have to remain chaste and homebound. They often fail to notice or admit how often they are criticized by other women, and kept in line by females' expectations of them, in addition to whatever restrictions men place upon them. Males justify their dominance and control over females by their own needs to protect women and keep them safe from harm. Many women want only to be provided for and taken care of, but most are told by the feminists to be completely independent and self supporting.

These are even further contradictory influences in girls' lives.

However, often women are mysterious to men because they are so to themselves. With so many different ideas being thrown at them constantly, it is no wonder that this is so. A typical girl may finally admit that she's too confused about life, and then hope and expect a boyfriend to make her happy and solve all of her problems for her. She will give sex to a male in exchange for security, and also expect him to be the perfect fantasy of the romance novels she has been raised on. She will want your time, attention, energy, and strength to make her feel much better about herself. Any phone calls, gifts, cards, compliments, and visits give you points to score and win with her. Anything you fail to do (which is inevitable) will cause you to lose points with her. They will deliberately test you with silliness and nonsense. If you give in-you fail! They will then lose all interest in you, because you are a wimp and not tough and self assured enough. You lose your ability to make them feel protected, and you lose your status with them. It's the way women are.

If you don't have a girlfriend yet, you will soon get one. Almost all single girls out there want boyfriends to make them happy and brag to the other females about. Since they want a prestigious male most of all, try to do something famous or successful. A new car, or job promotion, or, in my case sometimes, something published, will work wonders for you. One time I self published a little book of my own, and gave out copies to girls I wanted to impress and date. Many of them went out with me, and most of these eventually (if not sooner) let me get them into bed. I didn't have a steady job, or brand new car, but that little book sure helped.

Another time I did have a new car, and suddenly three different and attractive single young ladies wanted to go for rides in it. One even told me (repeatedly) about how "cool" I was in my car. Of course all three of them had envious female friends and co-workers to talk all about me with.

This too more than made up for my lack of a high paying and high status job.

I lacked a lot of self confidence because I wasn't at all rich, famous, or powerful, but I faked it. The new car and the girls' loud praises began to boost my ego. After that I was able to pretend to be dynamic and confident, and the "hero" type they wanted me to be.

Women are the same way, insecure and lacking in self confidence. They want and need a man in their lives to help them get over this problem. That is also why they find insecurity and lack of self-assurance in men such a negative characteristic. They have enough of their own problems, and they don't really want to be your mother. So even if you're not, summon up all the courage you can, and pretend that you are. No matter how much fear of shyness or rejection, ASK a girl out. If she says no, then realize that, even though it's crushing, you'll get over it. Move on to the next and the next ones, and keep asking. Sooner rather than later you'll have one say YES!

VII

Statistics

Remember: there's three females for every two males. They have biological clocks to worry about and you don't. And they have families and friends constantly pressuring them to get married that you don't. You have your car, job, sports, hobbies, male friends, classes, boat, or whatever in your life. Women usually do not. They are designed and raised to be birthing and nurturing maternal creatures. This is why most little girls play with dolls, like to cuddle stuffed toys and live house pets, and begin reading romance stories at so early an age. If you don't have a girlfriend you at least have your other things. But if they don't have a boyfriend they feel really left out. St. Valentine's Day for single and unattached women is an extremely sad, lonely, and depressing time of the year.

When a typical female is sad, lonely, and depressed she will often over eat, but many of them want and even need go shopping. It doesn't really matter what she actually buys, just as long as it's something for her. She will spend many hours in malls and clothing stores, looking longingly at window displays, trying on dresses or jewelry, just to see how she looks and feels with these on. Fashion markets thrive on females and their insecurities, and much of our economy is supported by cosmetics and frivolous consumer goods. There's another old saying: men think about things, and women feel about things. A female needs to feel that she is accomplishing something. Buying a new whatever helps her to feel somewhat better this way. But what she truly wants and needs is a MALE.

Women in colleges are now half of the student populations, but up to 50% of them do not finish and graduate. Many of them bug their boyfriends there incessantly, especially during times of exams and when term papers are due. You are there to get a B.A. or B.S. degree, but many females still are just there to get their MRS. degrees. I once asked a cute freshman girl in my college class what she was studying. She told me she was just there to be away from home so that her boyfriend would miss her. It apparently worked, as she dropped out to get married the next semester.

Girls who are absolutely desperate to get a husband, and there are many of them who are, will even resort to deliberately getting pregnant in order to finally "land a man." Throughout history there have been extremely high percentages of babies born months before the usual time after the wedding.

A humorous saying in many countries was that all babies take nine months to arrive, but the first one can come anytime much sooner than that. Other females may not want marriage exactly, but at least more of a permanent relationship. Sometimes if they willingly let males have sex with them, and then get too hurt, angry, and humiliated from getting dropped, they will seek revenge. Willing women will say they were raped, and the men find themselves in courts and jails, dazed and confused, for things they didn't really do.

Other women will do all they can to be provocative to get male attention, but then suddenly say that he harassed or molested them if others criticize those women as being too "loose" or "immoral." These women feel way too much stress from the pressures and expectations put upon them in our society, and lash back out by trying to protect themselves with accusing males of forcing them. Unfortunately the feminists, the legal system, and the prisons often do not understand this. It is no wonder that thanks to the new DNA testing, up to one third of all supposed rapists are getting their cases retried and dismissed. The seminal evidence is shown to not be theirs, and they finally get themselves released.

Once you get a steady girlfriend, things and life will begin to move along much more smoothly. She will be your best friend, bed partner, and use her feminity and sexuality to fine tune you to be and stay just the way she wants you to be. But after about a year she will suddenly start to change, and she feels justified to do so. She will want you to "commit to a more permanent relationship." This is her term for marriage. You have work, school, friends, family, and too many other concerns to deal with, but she will only get concerned about herself. She will argue, fight, stop giving you sex, and complain about you to all her girlfriends. You will no longer be the perfect male in her life as before, and all because you won't "commit."

This is, of course, super manipulation at its greatest. Each and every man has had to deal with this at one time or another. It is the reason marriage scares us so much, because it is the forerunner of what for too many men married life becomes. An aging, weight gaining, nagging, complaining, aggravating, irritating, and demanding wife we wish we were no longer tied down to. Men have the illusion of the attractive and undemanding woman who will satisfy all of our desires, and then disappear so that we can go and do other things for awhile. Some men actually find such a woman, but most do not.

There's also this anecdote about life: A young bull and an old bull were out on a hill together, and in the pasture below they saw a herd of cows grazing in the grass.

"Let's run down and get one of them!" the young bull exclaimed.

"Let's slowly WALK down and get ALL of them," the old bull replied. And so they did.

VIII

Just Beginning

But what if you don't have any kind of a girlfriend, and are not even close to getting a date with any female, anywhere, at all? Take the case of my friend Tim, a college educated and tall fellow in his early thirties.

"I keep trying, but just can't seem to score!" he complains.

There are probably a number of reasons for his not connecting, and for his repeatedly being turned down. And so we will discuss various scenarios and situations further in this chapter. In other words: you're new at it and/ or just starting out. Or you had one but lost her some-how, and want to try all over again, or whatever. Here are some ideas for you to think about: Women associate things differently than men do. For them sex (male lust) is love, or so they always hope. Money that men spend on them is the amount of love they are worth or not, especially in consumer U.S. society.

Yelling at females is paying some kind of attention to them, and many of them equate this with love as well. Often when you refuse something they have made or done, such as yet another helping of the same foods, they will fel personally rejected. You don't love them any-more. This can be a real problem, especially as females will make and keep it as such.

How can you overcome this? One way is to stop merely thinking just about your own personal problems and situation for awhile. Start paying attention to what her real situation is. Women will constantly drop hints about what they feel they want and need the man to say, be, and do. By paying more careful attention to what they are saying and how they are acting, a man can far better ideas as to how to interact with them.

I used to watch the actor Robert Culp in the "I Spy" television shows when I was a boy back in the 1960's. These were very informative, as his character always managed to get girls. He would pay attention to them, smile and be friendly, joke and tease them playfully, while constantly giving them compliments. But he was also firm with not standing for any of their feminine nonsense. They felt safe and secure with him, and enjoyed the status of being with this international tennis player hero.

I found that by behaving the exact same way with girls in my high-school in the 1970's, the exact same thing happened to me! I started getting a few girls to talk to me, and one or two to even go out with me.

I was considered tall, charming, attentive, and witty, and thus fun for them. I was too shy and awkward to try to grab or seduce them, and they thus considered me to be "safe" as well. They would brag to their girlfriends about the dates, and thus keep up with their peers. It was not perfect, and after awhile I found most of them quite boring, but it was an excellent way to get started and gain some practice.

In college I worked summer jobs in a furniture factory, and one summer I got some useful advice that was far better than any so called knowledge I paid tuition for. An older Black fellow, Joe, befriended me. He had come up from the South as a boy and had never gone to highschool, let alone college. But he'd had many life experiences, and especially tremendous interactions with females. I'd tell him about the difficulties of getting and keeping steady girlfriends, and of how much effort we younger guys would put into pursuing them. And especially how painful it was to lose them despite all our efforts to keep them.

Joe just smiled and told me, "Let the woman chose you, and you'll never have any trouble with her!"

In the Fall I was back on campus, and completely stopped chasing after the superficial coeds. In classes I'd drive them crazy by merely smiling and nodding at them, but never trying to initiate anything with them. Soon I had several of them competing against each other for my attention, and all of them wondering what was with me? I wasn't gay, but probably someone really "cool" since I was a little distant and aloof. In other words I was acting like I didn't want or need any females since

I probably had too many already. Finally I'd let one "impress" me enough, and drop enough hints to me about bars, movies, food, etc. to ask her out. Every time the girls would readily say, "Yes!" I got dates and sleep over companions regularly from then on.

Then there's ways to meet women through the singles bars or dating services. These sometimes payoff, but usually don't, but are still worth at least a half-hearted attempt. In the bars you can at least see instantly what she's like, whereas in the want ads classifieds sections of the Meet Market pages you have only brief descriptions to go on. There's also video dating services, where you get to screen a scripted and acted short performances. There are some common occurrences in these kinds of methods, especially in that it can cost too much money, and both genders run into a lot of fakes and phoneys. Many of the women lie about their true ages, and many of the men lie about their true marital situations.

If, after a few dates, you decide that it's time to have sex with her (which, of course you wanted to do right away. but wisely waited), go for it! You've been attentive and entertaining, all the while being sexy by talking about sexy things. You've given her enough compliments, not been crude or neglectful, but also been friendly to the other females who suddenly appeared all around. You've kept your hands mostly to yourself, and let her decide to come on to you. So you make your move.

You invite her out for a dinner, then your place for a drink. Your roommate is gone for the weekend visiting his family. The room becomes your lair, and she's there alone with you. You kiss and caress her, and wait for her to respond fully to you. Then you tell her how much you care about her, and tactfully ask (never begging or pleading!) if she'd like to spend the night. She will say yes, no, or maybe, depending on how she feels about you and her situation. If she says no, then do NOT get angry, and instead help her get home. If she says maybe, then ask her when and where, and wait for her to set things up. But if she repeatedly says no, then it's time to stop calling her for dates. There's plenty of other willing females out there.

You don't have to waste your time, energy, and money on ones who won't ultimately put out.

Women complain all the time about men who merely use them for sex, but for most of them these are exactly the kinds of males they are the most attracted to. You bring her candy, flowers, gifts, cards, dinners, time, attention, and respect. But she repays you with games, manipulation, and NO sex. She's beautiful, but really not worth it. Stop trying to date the near perfect model types, and go after the warmer and friendlier ones. The cute little one with glasses will surprise you! She will do what you want her to in order to keep going out with a nice and sexy guy like you.

Once in bed be an excellent lover. Lots of foreplay, holding, cuddling, kissing, fondling, etc. and not merely coital probings. Get some books and manuals on sexual techniques to learn all the details. The best ones seem to be by some old hippie medical types at any kind of research institute in California or somewhere similar. Soft lights, candles, music, and such go a long way to helping stimulate her auditory senses. She will be very worried about her naked appearance, her breast size, or her body weight. It goes without saying that you always assure her of how perfect she looks. Be strong, dominant, and in charge, while gentle and loving with her. She'll absolutely love it! It's exactly what she wants and needs from you in bed.

After sex never roll over and go to sleep, get up for a smoke, or stop being with her to answer the phone. Women hate this in men, and always complain about it. Yet so many guys never seem to figure out that this is not nice to do. She has just given you herself, and she certainly expects you to appreciate it. Always continue to kiss and caress her, and fall asleep eventually while holding her. This will make her feel completely loved and cared for, far less guilty about being there, and usually desiring to spend nights with you again.

Later dates can include hot tubs, body massages, nude beaches, nudist clubs, softcore adult videos, strip poker sessions, lingerie fashion shows, exotic modeling for your camera, and other kinds of wildly unusual things will always help you to score with her. These are highly useful to keep her interested in you. But be careful! After a few more dates you will find that she's starting to drop hints about marriage and children. She'll suddenly invite you to her sister's wedding as her "steady date" and make sure to introduce you to all her family and friends. She'll start to ask you about whether or not you like kids, what you were like as a boy, your family, etc. She's REALLY interested in you at this point!

So now you've got that enviable position to be in of getting to decide which girl you want to keep seeing, which one you want to continue bedding, and even eventually marry (if you want to do so). Lucky you! Before you had no girls at all, and now you suddenly have several. They suspect there are others in your life, and they are competing against them. The best girl is, of course, the one who begins to cater to you. She'll invite you to be with her, cook you your favorite foods, and have you enjoy her for dessert.

And all you had to do was wait them out, then ask them out, and then psych them out. You get and stay in control by letting them feel that they are in control of you. Perfect! The rest is all downhill. So enjoy.

One further note: don't get jealous when the other guys all start looking at and flirting with her. You've got her relaxed, aroused, and excited about being a woman. The other males sense this and want to admire her too. Just agree that she shouldn't get too jealous when you look at and flirt a little with the other females. After all, the two of you are now a sexy, mature, and sophisticated couple together. It's what life is really all about.

IX

First Date

There's girls everywhere, in school, church, clubs, work, super market grocery stores, and even in those singles' bars. You finally get up enough nerve to go up to her, the one smiling at you and dropping all the hints to you, introduce yourself (again) and ask her out. Lines and gimmicks don't work, and so you're honest and sincere. To your surprise she actually says YES! But now what do you actually do? Where do you go? And what happens?

"I really wish the guys could make all the right decisions about our dates, especially at first," says Karen, 24, a lovely chesty brunette.

"It would sure make things a lot easier if he knew what he was doing!

If he's nervous it's too much! I'm already nervous enough on my own!" says Jolene, 26, an attractive office temp.

Most women decide to let the man come up with where to go and what to do. It's all part of their romantic ideas about being pursued, wooed, and won. So make this work for you as well. There's couples and small groups dating for the first few times. Less pressure and less expectations. Then there's "platonic dating" where you're just friends going out together for only an occasional social event. And then there's REAL dating where you want what she has, and she has what you want, and you both know it, and you'll both negotiate for it, because she (eventually) wants you to have what you want.

A BIG SECRET WOMEN NEVER TELL MEN IS THAT THEY EACH WANT THE MAN TO LET THEM KNOW HOW THEY SHOULD BEHAVE! That way they will never offend him if they have decided that they like him enough to stay with him. If he wants her to dress and act sexy she will do so. If he wants her prim and proper she will adjust and behave accordingly. A woman wants a man to give her boundaries and limits within which to operate. Once she's able to figure out what it is you want her to be, she will become that for you. This way she always wins. So ask and/or tell her how you'd like her to dress and act, and give her compliments and approval in the meantime.

If you take her to a movie on the first date there's very little communication going on between you two. A better move is a meal. Then you can sit across from each othwer and get to know one another. Instead of a dinner, which will put her on her guard, meet for a nice lunch. She'll have an hour to evaluate you and decide if she wants to continue on. Then you can go for an afternoon walk, swim, drive, ride, or whatever. Be sure to be your best with enough of her girlfriends beforehand, as she'll be certain to get their opinions of you as well. Show up on time, with a flowering plant, neat and clean, with enough money.

First dates can be fun if you can keep yourself under control. She's going to be worried you might try something that she does indeed want some lucky fellow to ultimate do with her. But she does not want it to happen until she's ready for it. After all it's her body, her emotions, and her life she's considering. So before the date get your visual materials, your personal private place, and get your dynamic tensions out of your system.

This can be magazines in the bathroom, videos in the living room, or just your fantasies on top of your bed. Use either hand, or both hands, or whatever else is needed to get the job done.

Afterwards you will be somewhat calmer, and far more calming to her.

You won't be staring at her assets, even though she may be trying to show them off to you, in too blatant a way. You'll mostly keep your hands to yourself, and wait for her to take your arm, or rub her chest up against you, or sit in your lap, etc. She will indeed be doing these things, and so much more! soon enough, but probably not on the first date. It's true that some first dates can REALLY be surprising. I took out a girl from a place I had a temporary job at one time. We had dinner and drinks, and she invited me to her house.

She invited me in to watch a movie on tv, and excused herself to go to the bathroom. Soon after she re-appeared wearing a flimsy negligee, and piled up on me right there on her couch. I forgot what the movie was, but I well remember her. She invited me to stay the night, and, of course, I did just that. But these kinds of lucky occurrences are rare. Most end with just the proverbial handshake or kiss on the cheek. I'm fairly certain, though, that the reason she got so sexual so soon was because I said or did absolutely nothing to suggest anything like that. I was attentive and friendly with her, gave her compliments, and talked about what SHE was interested in. And so she decided to reward me in the very best way.

On the date don't talk about your favorite sports team, your job, your car, your friends, your opinions, or whatever. Ask her about hers. This will make you unique in her eyes because you'll be so much different, and so much better, than the other less enlightened guys she's gone out with.

You'll be different and much more fun to be with. She'll relax and begin to feel at ease with you. The next step for her is her feminine horniness to be held, kissed, cuddled, caressed, and ultimately made love to. But in the meantime she'll certainly appreciate your behaving yourself and waiting for her to get herself ready for it.

The first date will usually end itself when one or both of you is/are decided to do so. You may have other plans, or be tired, or have to get up early the next day. Take her home as far as her door and shake or kiss her hand goodbye. Tell her you had fun, and if she invites you in plan on just staying there for only a few minutes. Don't suddenly disappoint her with any changes in character or mood. Stay calm and yourself, as that is what she's gotten used to. If she invites you to stay fine, but don't expect it, don't ask for it, and don't even think about it. Women can read mens' minds in many ways.

Don't make the mistake I made with a gorgeous blond girl at school.

I took her to a movie and then said goodbye at her dorm door. Smooth enough, but I still ruined it by showing up twenty minutes early and without enough money to pay for both our tickets. I finished off myself by calling her twice right away and asking her out again. Of course she turned me down both times. It's so much better not to call her for a short while. You need to be too busy to merely be preoccupied with just her. Visit your family, friends, colleagues, or whatever. Maybe even take another girl out. After at least a week phone the primary female, leaving a message if you have to, just to chat. Don't ask her out again until the next call.

Even if you live in the same little town you can send her a greeting card with a nice note. Give her time to think about you from the safer distance of her own dwelling place. Without being arrogant or rude about it, merely make her wait a little while. Maybe even send her a gift, and wait for her to call you to say thanks. Listen carefully to any and all hints she'll give you about going out again. Then ask her, but don't expect a yes without an explanation as to her time limits. Second and third dates can be dinners or movies, or more romantic sessions in your or her place. Eventually she just may surprise you, and pleasantly so, with the gift of herself. ALL of herself!

If you want to have sex with her, and she keeps going out with you but rejecting you, there's something ultimately wrong. She wants your time, money, and attention, but not you yourself. After too many dates of nothing happening, merely cease calling her and ask the other girls out instead. They'll know all about you via the feminine grapevine, and it should be much easier to get one or two others to spend time with. Be your gentlemanly self with them for the first few times, and then begin to suggest more intimate activities. Hot tubs are an excellent third or fourth date, especially with wine and soft music. Eventually there will be one lovely lady who you like who will be your WOMAN exactly how, where, and when. Waiting was well worth it. Consider the other dates to have been preliminary and practice sessions.

We all have budget restrictions no matter how much we make. The bills will never stop coming. You'll have to keep within your limits, and don't go overboard with credit cards (no matter how beautiful she is).

If she just wants you for your money you're really wasting you time. It's better to let her know about how much you have on you, and let her decide to help you stay within that range. She'll have a few bucks of her own too, especially for cab fare in case she decides to leave you and go home alone. If she wants to help pay for the date let her. The feminists may be right there, at least in that way.

Eventually you'll have her spending nights, days, weekends, and even a lifetime with you. Remember that she wants you just as much as you want her, just as soon as she makes up her mind about you. And there's always the added pressures of competition for her. The other women she knows are going out on dates, getting engaged, married, having babies, etc. She does not ever want to be left out. And so she will eventually be there for you. Naked, aroused, pleasing, satisfying, contented, safe, and secure, in bed with you. A perfectly warm, willing, wanting, and sexual female. Yours. It was well worth the time, effort, self-discipline, and wait.

X

In Bed

In Asia sex is something that a woman does FOR a man. In Europe it is something that a man and a woman do WITH each other. But in America sex is something that a man does TO a woman. Each of these cultures have their own reasons for this, and in the United States human sexuality and sexual expression are among the most neurotic experiences on the planet. Each and every state has anti-nudity and anti-sexuality laws, which are strictly enforced. The American media thrives on sex scandals.

In any U.S. locality a movie or TV show having a woman bathing would be considered "dirty", even though she's washing herself thoroughly. But a man in a fight, with mud, dirt, and blood would be considered to be good "clean" wholesome family entertainment. How can getting clean be "dirty"?

And how can getting dirty be "clean"? There is no logical reason, except that American still subject themselves to negative feelings about sex.

Churches, parents, schools, and law enforcement officials constantly control us with guilt and remorse for our sexual desires.

Pornography and topless bars are kept well regulated and repressed, and are permitted only in certain areas for income and tax purposes.

Politicians can win or lose elections based upon their sexual behavior, sexual orientation, or personal reputations in such regards. Women in America are especially bombarded with tremendous amounts of contradictory messages regarding their sexuality. They are supposed to be attractive and sexy, while at the same time being virginal and non-threatening. So when you finally get your female in bed, or actually she gets you there, try to remember that she's been through a lot of stuff already in her life.

Always assure her that you care for her, that she's wonderful and desirable, and that you don't care if she's slightly overweight, not big breasted enough, wrong color haired, or that there's no more hymen membrane there anymore. Let her know how much you appreciate her being there with and for you, and always be sure to kiss, cuddle, and hold her before, during, and after sex. Get some sexual instruction manuals and read up on how best to fondle, caress, lick, chew, pinch, bite, probe, stroke, nibble, and maul. Learn about her erogenous zones, her clitoris, and her G-spot.

"So many guys are such clumsy oafs in bed! They don't know the first thing about a woman's body!" complains Jackie, 26, a red haired artist.

Don't be like all the other guys. Learn all you can first. And always ask her what she likes you to do, and tell her what you'd like her to do.

Always give her lots of extra time to get used to your desires, and take your time getting her warmed up for hers. She'll want you even more for it! You'll be truly unique. That special guy she'll want to hold on to and please and satisfy forever.

Picture books and magazines, and adult videos will give you lessons on anatomy and genitalia, body responses, and what to do. If, after awhile, you both find that you enjoy more heavy duty activities, like tying each other up or having groups watch you going at it, then have a good time with it all! Most girls will eventually pose naked for you, as they all have secret fantasies about being models. Just make sure she has a set of the photos and all of the negatives after each modeling session. Massages, candlelight, soft mood music, wine, and a gift of any kind of jewelry she can show off will always work with getting her exactly the way you want her to be.

I've had two lovely nude young ladies in a hot tub with me, after waiting for the two of them to get used to the idea, and assuring them both that I would not favor one over the other. Give each of them equal time and attention, and try not to make them jealous of each other, is the best policy with threesome situations. They were also best friends with each other, didn't mind kissing and hugging one another at all, and we all three found that it was well worth it! I've also had two naked young women on a nude beach in California, though I couldn't do too much with them there because of the public being all around. But it's truly amazing just how sexual and desiring females will be, if only we allow, help, and encourage them to be so. It's what we want. In bed it is precisely what she wants to happen that will happen. She wants and needs you to be strong, dominant, and protective, while also being sensitive, respectful, and persistent. She will allow, help, and encourage you to be so. It's what she wants.

Run your hands slowly bur surely all over her, and then ask her permission to remove a certain article of her clothing. Start with her shoes, hat, scarf, belt, or other such outer item. Then the blouse and bra.

She will absolutely love being topless for you, but only after you've given her enough time to get and stay sufficiently aroused with all the foreplay.

Remember to ALWAYS assure her how perfect her tits are, and those two mammaries may be breasts any other time, but in bed they're TITS and their there for you to enjoy! Both of them! Finally remove her skirt or pants, leaving on her panties for a later development. Have her undress you, and let her do all the work getting your clothes undone and off. She will be turned on by your body nudity, but not just by any specific part. You will especially want your favorite part(s) of her, but she will be most turned on by all of you.

The first night maybe just hold her, even if she finally gets her panties off one way or the other. If you were wise and gotten your dynamic tensions out of your personal system beforehand (using whatever hand), you will not be so wildly irresponsible to get off into her. She will certainly appreciate this in you, the really cool dude so totally unlike all the other guys she's dated. Wake up together and give her juice, toast, and tea in bed the next morning, and then see what happens. I had one sweet young thing tell me she wanted a "Sausage" for breakfast, and she didn't mean the kind you fry in a pan on top of the stove!

Go down on her first for a long, long time, and you're guaranteed to get and keep her moist and squirming for you. Let her take hold of your penis and insert it into wherever. I once had a girl actually begging me, saying "Please! Please!", to keep having sex with her while I was on and in her. She enjoyed it so much. She was also able to have multiple climaxes, and she was the one who would actually dig her fingernails into my back.

Another one always moaned loudly and continuously, and even threw her arms up over her head. Her large and firm breasts (those two tits!) stayed that way and she'd always bounce them around for me...including right smack dab into my face. Another one would buck and heave under me so fast and furious that I would be literally tossed out of her. There really are such lusty ladies out there! You'll find them. I finally did.

Another time I had a nice hot and horny young woman modeling sexy lingerie for me, and leaving bright red lipstick kiss marks all over my body. And I mean everywhere! Females have their sex drives and fantasies too. So make use of this. Just be patient and wait for her to decide to let you have her. After a few night times together, you can patiently move on to your own more specialized desires. You can hold her and watch a good X-rated video together, while comparing her favorably to ALL of the naked actresses on the screen. I have never had a girl refuse to let me use a vibrator on and in her, but only after I have waited enough of a while to let her get used to the idea.

As bed time proceeds along, you can really begin to get creative, and she will want to help you. Act out your fantasies! Enjoy the sensual pleasures of life and youth. Get her to wear nylon stockings and nothing else, or high heeled shoes and nothing else. All females have these in their wardrobes, so make use of them. She'll want to wear lots of makeup and jewelry for you. She'll want you to chase her all around the house, and deliberately let you catch her conveniently in the bedroom. Carry her around naked for awhile, and keep kissing her until she begs that you put her on the couch, floor, or mattress. Garter belts or leather items of apparel are many peoples' turn ons. Cover each other in whipped cream…licking it all off of each other. You may even get into handcuffs, enemas, or spankings with ping-pong paddles. Whatever you both enjoy is yours to enjoy. So enjoy!

Be creative in your fantasies. Dress up in exotic costumes like her in a topless belly dancer outfit. Or have her be a naked slave girl and buy her in an auction for your harem. She can dress up as a hooker and you can even pay her cash afterwards. A tight one piece swimsuit and bunny ears and tail can make her into a playboy bunny waitress to bring you your favorite beverage. On your birthday she may ask you, as one cute neighbor girl once did to me, what she can give you for a gift. Definitely tell her: HER!

Have her be naked and wrap herself up in ribbons, with balloons and a bottle of champagne. Let her have out her fantasies, as well. Give her equal time.

She may want you to be a pirate, prince, Zorro, Tarzan, a doctor, or a whatever. Let her have her way with you, too.

I once had a one night stand with a girl who loved to nibble and suck on my toes. Another one got off on my blowing and tonguing in her ear during coitus. One liked my fingers (though no more than three total) in her bottom when she was on top. The big chested loudly moaning one was also very oral and loved to taste and swallow. For her it was good to the last drop. One lady from New York whom I met in California (where else?) liked having her nipples pinched extremely hard. The oral one also climaxed whenever I'd bite into the back of her neck. She also enjoyed showing off the "hickie" marks to the other females……

The nipple pinching girl also liked to please me back by inserting her tongue all the way into my (clean) anal groove. All of the females I've kissed enjoyed "French" tongue kissing, and none of them ever objected to hugging for no other reason than just to hug. There are various positions in all kinds of places. Her on top, sideways, backwards, upside down, etc.

The ancient Indian Kama Sutra book of erotic love will provide all sorts of illustrations for these. Get her out of bed once in awhile to make your day on porches, beaches, woods, cars, pool tables, pools, canoes, rafts, surfboards, hammocks, water beds, sailboats, and anything else available.

I've heard of couples doing it in airplanes, hot air balloons, elevators, taxi cabs, ferries, and even in the back seats of busses.

But never forget the most important rule of sexual intercourse with women. Always tell her before, during, and afterwards that you like her, appreciate her, and care for her. Females are auditory and emotional, and sex for them is always about love and affection. Keep her feeling sexual and desiring to please you. She's taking care of your physical needs, so take care of her sentimental ones. It's what life and love are all about.

Taking care of each other. Otherwise, you can continue staying home by yourself every night with nothing better to do than yank the crank. Think about it.

XI

Helpful Hints

1. Always be neat and clean, fairly well dressed, teeth brushed, and organized.

2. Be friendly and approachable, without seeming to be out on the prowl for them.

3. Never ask them out immediately, and always be friendly to the other girls with them. They'll be comparing notes after you've left.

4. Let them behave provocatively with you, giving you many obvious hints about going out, before you actually ask them out.

5. Don't expect to get the Perfect 10 one right away. Build up your dating abilities and self-confidence by going out with the average ones for a while. Females network, and your reputation will preceed you with them. Soon enough, the one you really want will have heard enough about you to begin to be interested enough to check you out for herself.

6. Never ever try to get your date in bed right away. Always wait awhile. Let her make the moves on you. She'll start rubbing her chest on your arm, or kissing your cheek, or running her hand on your leg, etc. soon enough. She's horny too, but she just wants to make you wait awhile to be sure about you. Remember too: she's fully aware of the other females eyeing you hungrily when she's with you.

7. Once you get her ready for bed, don't make it obvious that you set the whole thing up. Don't have your condoms lying around, but instead hide them and say that you don't have any. Be sure to check for your roommate's ones if the situation arises, and you can suddenly find "his" where you had them stashed.

8. Keep her well lubricated with wine, body oils, and compliments. Females are more auditory and olfactory: they hear, sense, and smell much more accutely than we do. They respond to music, soft lighting,

fragrances, and the sounds of our voices. They absolutely love it when we touch them, when and where and how they want us to.

9. Don't expect her to be a virgin, and if she's older she may also even have a youngster of her own at home.

10. Keep her interested in you with calls, cards, flowers, and lots of communication, especially to where she works (so her female co-workers will be envious and her status further increased, thanks to you).

11. Listen (Really Listen!) to what she is trying to tell you. Have her be more important to you than the game on TV or your buddies. Make her feel that she is the one single most important aspect in your life (after yourself).

12. Never hit her or abuse her in any way. Never force her to have sex, and never brag about what she's like in bed to anyone else. Protect her and her reputation, and tell her you will. She will absolutely adore you for it!

13. When she tests you with her games about how much she can get away with, merely smile and stop communicating with her. Leave or suggest that she date some other fellow. This will surprise her, and let her know that you are someone she can depend on to be strong and tough enough to keep her protected and safe.

14. Try not to whine and pout like a little boy with her. She does not want to be your mother. When she argues about whatever nonsense she feels she has to with you, merely agree with her in principle and wait her out. She usually just wants more attention.

15. When it's PMS time and she's REALLY wound up, there is absolutely NOTHING you can say or do to make her feel better about herself. Everything is wrong and all of your life is endless mistakes. But if you wait two weeks she'll be ovulating and at her sexiest. This is the perfect and sensual time when a woman is the absolute most fun.

16. The famous modern mythologist Joseph Campbell summed men and women up with this idea: In all cultures and eras men have had to DO something in order to accomplish and achieve their goals. Women

have merely had to BE attractive and desirable. You will need to go out and make yourself noteworthy, and she will make herself lovely and noticeable for you. While you compete against other males for position and place, she will be competing against other females for beauty and reproductivity. Understand and make use of these basic concepts.

17. Try to be the one "in charge" of things, while letting her think she can mold you into that almost Perfect Man she's always wanted. Tactfully make comments and suggestions to her as you proceed along as to how she can be more the woman of your secret desires.

18. Don't let yourself become boring or too predictable for her. Keep her guessing as to what you like and what you want to do. Be spontaneous and creative, especially by getting your friends and associates to help you with new ideas of what to do. Keep life with her fun.

19. Go out with another female every once in awhile, just to remind yourself that the steady one you already have is so much better than most of the other girls out there.

20. Be the first one to apologize, without giving completely in, after you have a fight. You can thus stay in control of the situation by letting her feel that she is right (as ususal), and you are sorry for being "wrong" (again). Soon after she will feel guilty about not being sorry first and will make it up to you in other ways. Your reward for your proper behavior will be HER. She wants you to have it, and will give it to you. The secret is to have her continue to feel that it is always on her terms (while they're in actuality on yours).

21. Always try to be sensitive and caring, while at the same time strong and protective. Try not to ever be wimpy or childlike, selfish or spoiled, or abusive. Women respect a man who can and will take care of them way more than one they have to take care of.

22. Try to always give the impression that you are successful and somewhat accomplished, at something or anything. Women seek status in men, and the more trophies, ribbons, awards, promotions, medals, publications, diplomas, and certificates you can get the better.

23. After the first date don't call her right away. Let her wait a few days and then just make a courtesy call to tell her how much you enjoyed it. Wait a few days more and then call her to ask her out again, sometime. Society custom and tradition has it where the male is in charge of contacting the female. Take advantage and make use of this.

24. If she turns you down, simply ask another girl out. Keep asking, no matter how much trouble this is, until one says yes. You've got to ask! There simply is no other way. In almost all cases the females are still flattered that you at least tried.

25. Try to use her name a little more frequently when you speak with her. Women love the acknowledgment of their own names.

26. Talk about sex and sexual things in an indirect way with her, by mentioning others. But do not actually say or try to do anything with HER right away. This will make her realize that you are a suave and sexy guy, and not one to be uncomfortable with. The actual sex will come later, after she's thought about it, and will then be "her" idea.

27. If you meet a woman in a bar chances are she's a social drinker; if in a church she's a religious type; if in a school an academic type; if at the beach an outdoors type; if at a club a joiner; and through family a kind that relations think you should associate with. The best way to meet women is through friends, and especially through other women.

28. Some females are "daddy's girls" and many are more attracted to men who remind them of their fathers. Many women grow up in families where dad is all important in that he solves their problems, has all the answers for them, fixes things, and gives them money, clothes, toys, and his attention. If you are older and physically resemble her father you will often have an extremely significant advantage with her. If he had a beard or moustache, and you have one, chances are she'll like your appearance more. She'll like you better, faster, and easier.

29. Some females are attracted to younger men. They feel more nurturing and mothering, even to the point of being smothering, and feel younger themselves with these fellows. If you want a mommy or a more

mature woman (with a lot more experience!) try for this type. She'll certainly appreciate your caring concern, and reward you well for it.

30. Always be classy. Develop and maintain a sense of style with a real personal integrity. Say what you mean, do what you say, and never be a an untrustworthy fake or phoney. Women adore class. It's so rare nowadays. You'll be the most special man around.

31. A major difference between males and females is caused by their internal chemicals: testosterone and estrogen. The former causes men to be more active and aggressive. The latter causes women to be more passive but also depressed somewhat more easily. This is why so many females seem to enjoy hearing and reading about how bad, sad, and lonely other womens' lives are. "Misery loves company" is how the old saying goes. (Studies of this have been done by Dr. Laura Schlessinger). Thus so many girls need constant reassurance for their insecurities, and someone good like you to help and keep them cheered up. Pay positive attention to them!

32. And always remember: there are three females for every two "suitable" males. Take advantage of these odds. They're always in your favor. You hold all the cards, and it's your game. So play to win. Go for it!

XII

Breaking Up

Divorces occur now at an over 50% rate nationwide, and at 60% in such states as California where the lifestyle is more transient and transparent.

Breakups for males and females engaged, living together, or just going steady occur at even higher rates. Most of us date and get intimate with more than one boy or girl before getting married. Money is always an issue, especially in Capitalist and consumer orientated America. Even if a woman makes more money that you do, she will still expect you to pay for things (and despite the fact that you're flat broke). Every male knows that females are expensive and high maintenance items to accommodate and care for. Dates which include dinner, drinks, a show, a gift, and whatever else can really eat into a guy's paycheck. And the outcome is always a gamble filled with uncertainty.

If she only shakes your hand goodnight, then closes and locks her door, you can drive home wondering what you did wrong. One young woman told me that the problem wasn't with me...it was with her (whatever that meant).

Another one came to visit me for supper, ate, told me that she would like to stay with me but I was "too nice", and left. If you do get naked in bed with her she will often be somewhat un-responding, worrying about her body appearance or breasts size, especially the first time (with you). You can keep trying to reassure her that you care for her, she looks fine, etc. But dating women to get sexual release is always a risky undertaking.

With all the dating nonsense and confusion that never seems to clear, it is no wonder that many men prefer doing much more simplified visits just with prostitutes instead of bothering with wives or girlfriends. They figure that they end up spending about the same amount of money, but that they get the desired end result in a much quicker amount of time. And it is both definite and without all the entanglements and other endless complications involved. It is relatively easy to get a female who strongly desires to be with you, but it can be very difficult to get rid of her if you desire a different one instead. And they can feel the same way about us.

For the same reasons of your wealth, power, and status being so attractive to women, the lack of these makes you unattractive to them.

You will find that quite often if you lose your job, have no money, move farther apart, no longer have as much time to spend with them, or any other such lessening thing, you will also begin to lose them. Many of them will decide that you are no longer "marriage material" after all, especially if their female fiends and co-workers criticize and denounce you to them. You are no longer the steady and worthwhile provider of status and security for them. They no longer want to give you sex to manipulate your behavior, as you are a waste of time for them. They will try to go after another man with better career and provider prospects instead.

Whenever I experienced periods of unemployment, whatever girlfriend I had also seemed to vanish. Two cases really come to mind, and both where the fiances each made the separate decision to drop me. The first one, a multiply orgasmic Jeanne, told me that I was definitely a Chauvinist.

She decided to have a fight about her not eating bananas because flies supposedly laid eggs on them. This, of course made no actual sense, since everyone peels away the skins before eating them, but she was in no mood to make logical sense. I wrote her a long goodbye letter telling her how much I'd appreciated her Feminist talents, ideas, and abilities.

The second one was a full chested and loudly moaning Jane, who left me for a nerdy little fellow with a steady high income job. She said that I was definitely NOT a Chauvinist, but decided instead to have a fight about Darwinism. According to her Charles Darwin was a fraud who got all of his evolution ideas from others. I tried to tell her about his voyages in the Pacific and scientific studies, but she was in no mood for rational explanations. I wrote her a farewell letter telling her how much I'd appreciated her Traditionalism, and left her a book on Darwin's life and achievements as a parting gift. I survived these ordeals, but after each split I certainly felt very, very saddened for a long, long time.

Breaking up hurts deeply and terribly. Divorces frequently occur soon after a husband gets terminated or laid off from his job, or when the wife finds out he's had an affair. The IRS confirms that 80% of its successful audits and prosecutions of men cheating on their taxes come about because of information suddenly supplied from their ex-wives. Womens' magazines advise them to let their boyfriends down easy when they want to stop dating them. But this is seldom the way it actually goes. As the old song goes, breaking up is hard to do. But do it if you must, get over it as quickly as you can, and get back into The Game again. There's plenty more of young, single, attractive, desirable, warm, friendly, and willing women out there.

After Word

All you have to do is go after them. Despite all their faults, they're still worth it. After all, you can't stay home and scratch your own itch forever. There's always at least one girl somewhere who will do it for you.

And, guaranteed, there's plenty of them who want to do nothing else but please and satisfy your needs. That's what they're for, and that's what they'll do. Just try and understand why they're doing it. Think about how frightened, worried, pressured, and confused they are by all of the many contradictions they have to face. Help them to cope by being what they want and need you to be, and get yourself in bed with them most easily by making them think they may have to compete against other females for you. You are the super cool and worthwhile one. And remember: Knowledge is Power.

This information will provide you with some, though by no means all, that there is to know about women. But it should at least help you to understand and cope with the female of the species more easily. So make your new found awareness about women work for you. Be patient and attentive to your date, but don't take any B S from any of them. Good luck and good hunting! You certainly deserve it.

Appendix I: What If You Died?

What would your spouse or significant other do if you suddenly died? We asked area residents this question:

"I wouldn't know what he'd do!" says Kelly F., 36, a hair stylist.

"We've been married for five years now. But I haven't really thought about it."

"He'd take the insurance money and move to Florida", says Joyce Z., 31, a health therapist. "He'd really get off on all the babes down there."

Brian J., 43, a community education instructor, says "My wife would probably just get remarried to somebody from our church."

"She'd definitely miss me, or so she's told me", says Rick V., 32, a construction worker. "She's my homey and we're supposed to get engaged this Fall."

"I know that he'd be sad for awhile, but he'd probably just go out and find a newer model", says Jennifer G., 44, housekeeper and mother.

"We've been married for nine years now, with two kids, a dog, a cat, and a hamster. "That's a morbid question, you know!"

Some we asked declined to answer, and some just laughed and replied with jokes about undertakers overcharging for funerals. But most answered honestly and truthfully, providing thought provoking ideas:

"I've been with him, off and on, for six months now", says Cherie D., 21, a college student. "He'd probably just ask my best friend out instead. And you know what? She'd probably go out with him. The bitch!"

"My wife wouldn't care if I croaked. We're getting a divorce anyways", says Mike F., 26, a mechanic. "But my girlfriend would miss me."

"I don't have to answer that. Stop bothering me with personal stuff", Kelli Peterman, 19, a store clerk told us. "I don't have a boyfriend any-more, anyways, so it doesn't really matter. Does it?"

"I don't like guys anymore. I just go out with my girlfriends now", says Jane D., 32, a delivery service receptionist. "But they'd cry and miss me, at least for awhile."

"Who knows what she'd do?" says Bob Z., 48, a production worker.

"My kids would be without a daddy, but the ol' lady could do anything."

"My dog would be lonely", says Michelle Q., 17, a high school student. "I don't have a boyfriend. I wish! Then maybe someone would care."

Steve F., 30, unemployed, says, "Who gives a rip about me? Why don't you ask me about the game?"

Jodie B., 35, a secretary says, "I just met this wonderful guy, and I hope that I'll be around for awhile to get to know him better."

Dave H., 51, an artist, simply said, "None of your business, man."

Most of the replies were ones about the personal and emotional aspects of the interviewees lives. But some covered other kinds of things:

"I hope I don't die anytime soon!" says Vicki T., 26, a sales assistant. "My stupid ho boyfriend owes me a lot of money. What would my little boy do?"

"She'd take my car, credit cards, and wipe out my bank account," says Chuck H., 44, a store manager. "She'd be gone before the funeral service was through."

Lyle P., 20, says "My girlfriend just told me she's pregnant. Man, what a question! If the baby's mine, then there'd be no papa around for it.

Good question. I'd better be careful and last for awhile."

"I don't really care, babe!" says Carla R., 20's, "He doesn't like me anymore, anyways, he told me. So just go away and leave me alone, thank you."

Most of us are indeed connected to others we care about, and who care about us. And, for most of us, if we suddenly departed from the

Earthly scene there would be a gap in each of those lives of the others with and around us.

Life for them would go on, of course, but we are all important and significant, each and every one of us in his or her own way.

Jill F., 41, a secretary, says, "Dude! I'd miss him almost as much as I'd miss my dog!"

Bree J., 16, a student, says, "Well it really doesn't matter because we just broke up. He didn't like my new henna design, and I like totally hated his stupid skull tattoo!"

"Dang, man! If she kicked off I'd have to marry this other lady I'm seeing on the side!" says Art, 46, who wouldn't give us his last name.

"I'd got it so she and the kids would be set for life. Everything's insured, including me", says Dave D., 52, a carpenter.

"She's always bitchin' at me to quit smoking. I guess she wants me to last for awhile", says Steve T., 61, a production worker. "Hey, maybe someday I will. I know they're really bad for you. I guess she cares......"

Whether we realize it or not, others need us and depend upon us to help make their lives more meaningful and worthwhile. So let's not disappoint any of them. Let's be more careful how we live our own lives. And let's all be around for awhile to still be a part of theirs.

And oh, by the way, what would your significant other do?

Appendix II: *F E M A L E S P E A K*

One of the neatest things about women is when they finally allow us to get them into bed. But one of the most confusing things about them is their word usage when this finally does happen. When girls are by themselves, and there's no guys around, they are just as crude and horny sounding as we are when we're out with the boys. But when they get with us they seem to clean up their act, clam up, and behave and speak in incredibly prim and proper ways. This is perhaps to convince us that even though they look and act like the sexy sluts we want them to be, they are not really that way, in case we don't ultimately want them to be that way, at the same time. (Or something like that).

When they're not experiencing their insecurities, and when they're not playing their usual attention, interruption, and manipulation games, women can really be a load of fun to have around. Talking to/with them can be a real problem though, and so we want to try to clear up as much of the vast confusion about their bedroom talk as possible. We have thus compiled a list of current common sexual terminology, in both English and idiomatic word expression, with linguistical translation into modern American "femalese." These also include what your woman will say to her lady friends when they're away from men. And you'd better believe that what they're talking about is most definitely you!

Anatomy

English	Slang	Female
anus	asshole	not there
breasts	boobs/tits	these
buttocks	ass/butt	back here
clitoris	clit	that
Grafenwohl area	G-spot	that's it!
hymen	maidenhead	it's bleeding! there's blood!
nipples	teats	them
penis	cock/dick/prick	it
pubic hair	bush	this
testicles	balls	those
vagina	cunt/pussy	there

Activity

English	Slang	Female
anal sex	back door	in my rear end
anger	piss off	he upset me (again)
apologize	made up	he finally said he was sorry
argument	fight	I'm mad at him again
arousal (hers)	moist/wet	he turned me on
attentive	lustful	I like him, he makes me laugh
betrothal	get engaged	see my ring
birth control	The Pill	you can finish inside me
boredom	time to move on	don't you love me anymore?
breast feeding	cream in your coffee	you can have both
caress	cop a feel	he put his hands on me
coitus	fuck/screw	sleep with him

complain	bitch	it's all his fault (again)
cunnilingus	eat out/go down	kiss me there
disease free	clean	you can have me
divorce	split up	he's available again
ejaculate	cum/goo	that came out of him
erection	stiffy	he got hard
fellatio	suck/give head/ go down	take him in my mouth
genital sex	go all the way	put it in
giving birth	popping out	it's time
hug	grab	he held me
humiliate	dump on	he doesn't take me seriously
hurt	kick her ass	he's really a nice guy
intoxication	get drunk	I didn't have that much
kissing	smooch	let him kiss me
masturbate	jack off/hand job	give him a full body massage

nurturing	giving of herself	all my love
oral sex	blow job	ok, I'll swallow
orgasm (hers)	cum/peak	made me climax
pornography	X-rated/adult	I would never do anything like that!
pose	expose herself	good form
pregnancy	knocked up	I think we've got a problem
proposition	wanna?	if you love me
prostitution	call girl/hooker/ whore/working girl	escort service
rejection	get rid of her	but he said he loved me
satisfaction	drained	he loves me
separate	break up	he dropped me
sex	do it	make love
shopping	shopaholic	women need to
swallow	gulp it down	it tastes like salty almonds
threesome	three way	ok, just this once

undress	striptease	dance for him
uninhibited	wild/out of control	I'm not really like that
vibrator	dildo	personal massager
virginity	maidenhead	aouw, it hurts!

Appearance

English	Slang	Female
beautiful	babe	nice dress
big	well hung	he's really big!
body	a piece	my figure
bottomless	bare assed	I'm not wearing any panties
bust line	her top	they're not very big
cute	baby	I was a really cute baby
handsome	what a hunk	he's good looking
heavy	fat	gained weight
height (his)	piled that high	wow, you're tall!
lactating mammaries	milk jugs	they got bigger
lovely legs	gateway to paradise	I shaved them
menstruation	period	that time of the month

muscles	body building	his big shoulders
naked/nude	nasty	he undressed me
ovulation	she's rarin' to go	I'm REALLY horny!
P.M.S.	on the rag	bad hair day
pretty	foxy	he said I looked like a model
sexless	dumpy	she's better looking than me
sexy	sleazy	stylish
suntan	get tanned	do you like my tan lines?
topless	tits sticking out	I'm not wearing a bra
ugly	dog	feel unattractive
water weight gain	bloated	do I look fat?

Other

English	Slang	Female
affirmative	go for it!	yes
apartment	her/your place	come in
bachelor	single guy	he's available
bachelorette	single girl	she hasn't found a husband yet
bd/sm	kinky sex	too weird for me
bisexual	ac/dc	I like both
bride	no longer jail bait	oh, look at her dress!
clothes	duds	fashion
condom	rubber	he used his protection
consensual	she's willing	you can stay here tonight
courtship	dating	go out with him
desire/lust	hots	passion

dominant	on top	he took control
employed	got a job	he's marriage material
enema	water sports	there in back
entertaining	humorous	he makes me laugh
famous	he made it	oh wow!
fetish	bent/kink	strange
frustration (his)	blue balls	he's too nice
heterosexual	straight	go out with him
homosexual	gay	we're just friends
husband	sucker	what a guy!
makeup (hers)	face paint	I'm still getting ready
marriage	get hitched	finally land a man
maternal instinct	she wants a baby	my biological clock keeps ticking
meet	hit on	he introduced himself to me
meeting place	meat market/ pick up joint	nice place

negative	no way!	no
new car	your wheels	he's so cool!
older men	lechers	they're so much more mature
penetration	get it in	give myself to him
proposal	ask for her hand	he respects me
rape	bop/gang bang	forced himself/ themselves on me
repression (hers)	neurotic	I'd feel guilty
rich	money bags	he's successful
roommate	roomie	gone for the weekend
seduce	score	he swept me off my feet
self conscious	she's uptight	they're all looking at me (again)
semen	jism	white sticky stuff
submissive	on the bottom	he makes me feel so secure
unemployed	out of work	he's a loser
underage	do hard time	I'm almost legal

| vulnerability | she left herself wide open | I trust him |
| wife | better half/ ol' lady | I didn't know he was married |

So memorize, utilize, and you'll be much better at communicating with her.

And never forget that wise and ever true saying: Knowledge is Power!

Appendix III: FINAL NOTE

This little book is a collection of ideas that have truthfully proven useful and successful. But it must be remembered that each female is a unique individual, and no two are exactly alike. You must first determine what kind of a woman you want, what exactly you want her for, and just what you are going to do with her once you get her. Do you want a friend and companion, or a business partner? Do you want kinky deep throat fellatio and/or anal sex in bed? Do you want a housemaid and cook? Or do you want a wife and mother of your children? Or any and all of the above? Both the original and final decisions are yours to make.

The ideas you have read should be studied and learned from over and over again. Most of them will be somewhat useful to you, and some of them will be exactly what applies to your specific situation. The single most important factor in handling women is that you must strive after them, no matter what. The later 1800's Irish playwrite Oscar Wilde made his famous play "The Importance of Being Earnest" about a man named Ernest. The fellow learned that women loved his enthusiasm for them. His eagerness to go after them. They responded to his intense and honest desire for them.

When it comes to females, your strength, self-assurance, persistence, perseverance, and patience will get you anywhere and everywhere. The comedy actor Woody Allen (Koningsberg) once said that 80% of success is just showing up. But by that he also meant that you actually have to do it in the first place. So get up and get at it. Good luck and good hunting!

And please write me and let me know how things turned out. Any comments, further ideas, and opinions would be most appreciated. Thank you, and live long and prosper.

Jeff Redmond
6475-28th St SE #266
Cascade MI 49546-6917

Suggested Further Study Materials

Allen, Woody (Koningsberg). Four Films of Woody Allen; Random House, NY,1982.

_____. Play It Again, Sam; French, NY, 1969.

Benayoun, Robert. The Films of Woody Allen; Harmony, NY, 1987.

Bjorkman, Stig. Woody Allen On Woody Allen; Grove, NY, 1993.

Campbell, Joseph. "Mythos"; Inner Dimension video series, NY, 1997.

_____. "World of Joseph Campbell"; Public Media video series, Concord MA, 1989.

Conner, Stanley. How To Find, Pick-Up, and Seduce Girls; Dynamic Distributors, NY, 1976.

Cousineau, Phil. The World of Joseph Campbell; Harper and Row, San Francisco, 1990.

Fisher, Helen. "Anatomy of Love"; TBS Productions, video series, 1995.

Gray, John. Men Are From Mars-Women Are From Venus; Harper-Collins, NY,1992.

_____. "Men Are From Mars-Women Are From Venus"; Genesis Media Group video series, Commerce CA, 1997.

Hicks, Roger and Victoria Day. The Joy of Sensual Massage; Wardlock, London, 1994.

Inkeles, Gordon. The New Sensual Massage; Bantam, NY, 1992.

Morris, Desmond. "The Human Animal"; Time-Life Video series, NY, 1995.

Moyers, Bill. "Joseph Campbell and the Power of Myth"; Mystic Fire Video series, NY, 1991.

Thomas, Patti. Recreational Sex; Peppermint, Cleveland, 1997.

Unseld-Baumanns, Christine. Erotic Partner Massage; Sterling, NY, 1990.

Vatsyayana, M. Kama Sutra (illustrated); Harper-Collins, NY, 1993.

Wilde, Oscar. "The Importance Of Being Earnest", The Complete Oscar Wilde; Quality, NY, 1996.

Wildwood, Chrissie. Erotic Aromatherapy; Sterling, NY, 1994.

About the Author

Jeff Redmond was born in Detroit and grew up in Grand Rapids, Michigan. He has attended colleges at Davenport College, Michigan State University, U.C.L.A., and Lund Universitet in Sweden, among others. He has bachelors degrees in History (with minors in Psychology and Education), Business Administration, and International Business, and a Masters Degree in History. He has worked in factories, school classrooms, river boats, corporate buildings, airports, publication places, college academic centers, governmental bureaucracies, and home offices. His military service includes time spent in both army and navy reserves.

Jeff is currently a columnist and news reporter for various newspapers, and a freelance writer for magazines. He has also written several books of both fiction and non-fiction. He is a member of the Authors Guild, the Authors League of America, the Freelance Editorial Association, the National Writers Association, the National Writers Union, the Society of Professional Journalists, and the Writers Guild of America.

He is a world traveler and has had many interactions with people from all kinds of places and backgrounds. These have included most continental U.S. states and Hawaii, India, Australia, North Africa, Scandinavia and Western Europe, Panama, Canada, and Mexico. Jeff speaks several languages, and enjoys researching and writing about his numerous trips and experiences. His chief love is to help others to improve their lives, and to offer them all the encouragement he can.